Behind My Rambling Eyes

Kathryn Dunphy

BookLeaf Publishing

India | USA | UK

Presentation by *BookLeaf Publishing*

Web: www.bookleafpub.com

E-mail: info@bookleafpub.com

ISBN: 9789358367256

First edition 2024

PREFACE

Exploring the notion of an emotional quality outside the range of normal human experience.

Contents

When in doubt; check your watch. ... 1
Melodrama ... 2
The Aliens ... 3
From Time to Time ... 4
Modern Curse ... 5
Mi vida escargot ... 6
Spy Juice ... 7
Doogie Raecy ... 10
At Crazy Camp ... 11
Those Life Tokens ... 12
It's When He Calls Her ... 14
Round Room ... 15
And It's True ... 16
Garments Off ... 18
Dream Lover ... 21
Letter ... 22
Couch Crawls ... 23
Don't Call Me A Trigger ... 27
Why Wonder ... 30
Maladjusted ... 32
Bowing Out ... 33

When in doubt; check your watch.

It's the pink lights
Creating a connect the dots
Wiping out the tears from my eyes

When it's meant to be it will
Worry no more
Why it feels like forever
It's just a drop of time

Melodrama

I give up on you
Of course you understand
You say you never knew

Thanks for clarity
Your naivety
I'll fall off balance
As you fail to ground me

The Aliens

3

Traveled too long and far too far to rest one's
head and hits it hard
Though the ambulance screamed it only left a
scar
I never stutter
I'll show you one day
Went a little too far
Rearrange the aperture
¿Qué dijiste?
It's only apropos

From Time to Time

It's like watching a year fall and thinking about gravity instead of considering my state of mind.

Modern Curse

You narrowed in
Positioning your importance
Right above my apparent lack

The invisible laughs of disgust
At anything I'm worth
Some candy to chew
But now it hurts your back tooth

Short skirts, crow's feet
Washed up tart
A harlot
Utter skank
Not the kind you bring home to mama
Would only add to your daddy's disappointment
So disappointed in you

Oi, to hell with such values!

So, what's worse?
An ass on backwards
Or, living with the modern curse?

Mi vida escargot

Oh well well well when we all fall down we'll
all go to hell
But from whence we came you'll remember my
name and eat ivy yet a feeling you dare forget
for a mist in the clouds and a dream in your
pipes
Sing light sing story light, a starry night

I saw myself dead and chained to a bed
Don't leave me he cries and ignores time passes
by so time after time the flute sings the lime
while salt plays a rhyme to a tune so soon now
remember

Howls and haunts with feelings to taunt

Spy Juice

Evil eye, evil guy. Who really cares.
Wafe of a man, should you recognize him in the
street. Frail and sickly, sunken eyes he carries
weighted defeat, and shuffles his feet.
You may hear sounds from his mouth, some
muttered and others loud. He'll step forth on a
platform of superiority. Why, he's quite
educated; he simply can't breathe. Wait around
for a moment, should you dare - or even produce
any small bit one might reckon is called care.
Easily missed while standing in the spotlight.
Yes, he blends into the dullest haze. This is
where he'll stay so invisible for all of his days.
Pathetic doesn't quite capture it, this man, a
littlest shit.
Don't misunderstand, he's quite intoxicating.
And if not merely for his sneaky ways of getting
you intoxicated. See, he thinks he's on a map of
liberated. His proximity has his wits far sedated.
He's much confused and nonresponsive to being
masturbated.
This mess of a man who no one will ever care to
understand trips as he falls down the biohazard
sewer.

The ache of his soul in which he is helpless to
untoil can be seen in his bright eyes while
dawning his beautiful smile. A snail.
Why now has it that my tone has changed? I
suggest it's him, now you suppose it's I'm who's
deranged? No, now, no, my dear.

As you see, without pride I must admit, I caught
a glimpse of him once and now pinch him
underneath his skin. I must promise you again,
my mind is quite clear, and I apologize for the
blips of trouble I possess after genetic digesting.

Watch me

His aches and cries he moans throughout the
night all alone in his room covered in a bed full
of lies. Quite contrived and dismayed, his aim to
ill-will shall drive you gutturally astray. Without
a seed of doubt are you to cast yourself as you
walk through him like you would a ghost in your
house. Though, he's most annoying as such that
of a rat's smallest louse.

Sprinkles on ice cream microwaved in feces was
his nightly dinner as a child. You'll smell it with
your ears. Woefully lost he wanders the dark
halls. With a life full of nothing, he spits out
dust.

Watch me

Harder….baby.

When is it we shall marry? Will we wear our tin
hats at the ceremony? Moan for me. Stay so
alone,

For me

Watch me. Can you see me? Tell me the most
beautiful of lies, honey. Take your honey, ugly.
You know you're scaring me. Heehee!

Doogie Raecy

It's with closed eyes I chose not to see
Every smile in you was one in me
It was hard not knowing
How your teeth don't fall
Out
Crying tears at you
Was much too high
A smile
For your life
In the years
Your teeth stood so still for

A smile in your heart
Already filled with tears
That any more
Might loosen the grip
Far too much
To slip back to those days
Silence was the most smile
To maintain hope
Between the miles and you
Getting to breathe
Again

At Crazy Camp

Yet when you flashed your fangs
It pissed me off. Well, I guess frustrated
I just told you I'd caught you earlier
That I knew you were a vampire
How I wasn't afraid of you

Then you smiled at me
Ever more confusing
Absurdly perplexing

I said I won't play your game
Oh, that beautiful smile
If those fools only knew
No, you won't trick me

Those Life Tokens

Those life tokens
What a joy
With
It will be
Now
As seeing which ones
So goldenly
Glee

Fear not a spree
To expense
As none too many
Must any possess

Mere dawning
Tokens
A rest

Fire lies
Eyes lay
With gloss gaze
We've token to forget
Reflecting fires
Every day
Tokens got
Cost

Hugging blows
Windows shatter
Viewed inside
From outside
Tattered walls
To open
Windows
Outside
Over covered
by
The blanket
Tokens lure

A golden tooth
To replace
Token tooth
To decay

Sly eyes
Disguise
The tokens tolled
For life
Where price gets
To forget

It's When He Calls Her

Get a hooker
Dolls on deliver
Is it over
Thank the heaven
Tell me politely
Knew you'd understand
He twirls in his chair, around
Mouth drops open
She just frowns
And loses focus
Face inside a phase
Locus of control

Round Room

15

DAMN ROUND ROOM
WHAT DID YOU DO
GIVE IT BACK WHAT YOU STOLE
FLIGHTS TO SIMULATED EXPERIENCES
WITH SOULS LONG GONE
FROM THE INSIDE OF THE POD THE
DOOR OPENS TO STRANGE
IS THIS DEATH
STUCK IN A DREAM
A COMA
THE FAKE ROOMS
THE SHOE BOX'S DESIGNED
STINGING WATER IN MY EYES

And It's True

And it's true
I want to be in love
To be loved
The exhilaration of new love
Desires for spontaneity
Passion and interest
An extra bounce in your step
How the sun always seems to shine
Curiosity that knows no end

But I don't have that
Days keep passing by
Relinquished to my bed
A greedy blank page
Nothingness so pervasive
An overwhelming weight to the day
No care for fresh air

Why can't I be in love with me
Encouraged to give me everything I need
To wink in the mirror
Flashing a mischievous smile
Knowing I'm love
And have been here all along

My brain runs on empty
Though I shove down the pills
The ones that work magic
It's all just frills
How hollow it is
To not feel a thing
Complaining proves nothing
And there's nothing to win

Try as I might
To convince myself there's something
I haven't caught the grip
It just seems to slip
Like the passing of days
In my makeshift grave

Garments Off

Garments off, all bets are lost. With our bodies intertwined, well, we never knew where to draw the line. There's never been a finer grace than to wake to your face with arms embraced, to feel happy I'm alive again. No, we aren't only friends, this cocktail of lust. Time and again it gets messed up and what luck we turn it all to "we just fucked."
Oh, honey, don't you know our hearts aren't cold and this feeling isn't bought and it can't be sold. An old perspective, how we messed up, kid. Precious souls, scared, bodies bare - happy to be here.

All bets are off, show me your guts. Braved it all before, stop showing me out. Aggressive, it's a blessing, though I've scared you away again.

Cuz all bets are off and this has never been only lust. Connections are fake and a sync can't be sunk, a grave so grave, we dive in, depraved. Wipe that look off your face, it's I who is amazed. Next to you, I feel renewed, and ready to moan our way to a brighter day with OJ fresh squeezed for two.

Who am I to beg? Who am I to talk, insist? A
kiss I want to kiss and feel forever astir. Explore
the world, explore me - her.

Who am I? Who am I? I lose my mind. Why
again now when I want to bring life, with our
eyes renewed into a small bloom. The child's
bedroom, sleeping one, made from two.
Not only love, ethereal - real.

Show me now, you won't back down. A strong
brew, hold my hand. Safe, the solace. Your
embrace, flawless.

Garments off.
Flame burnt, burst to dust. Lust, vehement love.
Garments off. Garments off.
Watch me unravel. Watch love rust. The rust
boils as it simmers, re-coil, embark my coil.
Seeds for spring, love isn't a ring. That feeling
begets, the past serves a lesson, my inner lining
burns desiring. Is the fire only for one, have you
left me where you left me? The love inside
swells, I'm unlike other girls. Anywhere in the
world is perfect right here. Blank stare, blue
eyes, take hands, life.

Garments off, a trace of lace, velvet lined and
grace. Intertwined, not displaced. Keep the looks
on our face, eyes locked, embraced.

With garments off, don't leave me, bring me
close - tell me to get lost. It was only a screw,
am I a fool's fool?

Dream Lover

If I had the power
You'd think of me
Tracing my jawline
Kissing my cheek
Holding me closely
Until I fall asleep

But until then
I'll have to pretend
You love me endlessly

For now I shall give my love to you
In my dreams
I dream so few
If you knew
You might love me too

Letter

The letter I'll never send
Will be the letter I'll never write
To you

Ever

Couch Crawls

And maybe that's just it. That part about herself she can't face herself. That part that hears how ugly she is instead of the words that are used. How it's an impossibility and eventually she'll have to face the reality that as she expected, she was too ugly like that. With a take no shit attitude she steps in the ring with her hands tied and her lips stitched up, all in order to protect her heart from the inevitable.

Stuck in a bubble where none of the good can be seen through her jaded disposition about her and her love. Taking a self-righteous defensive position so she can't melt into any embrace without her fear. Instead of enjoying the moment she hides herself desperately wishing to come out. Rejection only further affirms her deluded opinion of herself.

But it wasn't always like this. She had a good head about her once, before she lost herself in someone else. It became official and every comparison shown as the bleak possibility she could have to believe she really had a footing in the world, outcasting herself to cope with her

inability to ever make sense. She knew she
didn't come at every situation perfectly, but

She doesn't understand the chalked-out years
where she thought she was real. Or, how the
rolled-out carpet got swept out beneath her feet.
Rummaging through every second to see where
she went wrong, how she did it to herself.
Allowing herself to question the track record of
decisions she knew she had that make her great.

Yet, despite all that, you know she has that light
in her she won't let burn out. How she openly
yearns for connection with an unbounding
humility. Staking dignity even when she stakes
her tongue, she can admit she's wrong. How do
you tell her the ways you admire her? That she's
obviously so much that and to free her arms. Put
down her guard. Mostly the one she holds
against herself.

Looking into her eyes is the hardest part since
she's not afraid how they give it all away
because she can't be and she knows that. The
way she can hold you, take you in, let you be
seen. It makes sense why she's delightfully
surprised when someone asks her eye color. If
her smile so modestly shows her soul so vividly
displayed. Her ability to feel safe in the strangest

of ways. As though she can refer to the playbook
of every next line in the nick of time.

Is that why she asks so much? The way she
doesn't understand her beauty while comfortably
navigating the harder parts? Her at times dim wit
to dim-wittedness that pushes it pursuing ----

When you saw her standing there you got closer,
inches from her face, her body. You hadn't
expected of the exhilaration from so close. How
her eyes only warned you to the strength in her
tower that makes you weak in the knees.
Invigorating bliss. Grabbing her hands you
kissed her while tracing your fingers to her
shoulders and along her collarbone. Down her
breasts, catching her hips and pulling her to you.

Dialing back she's calling to see if you know if
you're a robot or not. Could it be aliens or an
overused product that's lost its luster? Is she
hearing that right, seeing it right?

Anyway, she's amazing with an unnerving depth
that'll take you in so fully you could easily feel
unhinged. How does she trust with such
unspoken respect? Or demand with utter lack?
How do you know who's wrong and is that ever
the point to joint freedom, to love? Then she

looks at you, knocking you back in reality. Back to where you remember that click, when you knew and you took a snapshot in your mind just for that reason. To love you you knew what she knew.

Magnifico!

Don't Call Me A Trigger

Could I write to the mystery
Of the online private diary
a word or two, of the day

See I'm sunken and depraved
at my awful ways
Reiterating what's been iterated, just to iterate

As you know
well as me
How to see altruistically
Though that's your job, not mine
I'm merely here to decline
Any inconvenience to mine
Oh, how she shines

I'll ask for you
To be my patient patient too
While I jigger with the white-washing of trigger

I won't let you own me
Lest stone you while you stone me
Though you don't owe me to hold me
That's that fine line between
Loving through hate

But do I know it can feel lonely
In a world rather bold to be
Inclined so awfully coldly
Oh my dear warm-hearted mate

It's exactly your beauty
That feels so ugly in me
While you dare me to be brave again

Won't you hold my hand in your hand
As I'm trying to stand
On my own two feet
My conceited plan

You owe me nothing
My sweet little muffin

But a shot rung in silence
Of ultra violence
Deploys my style, since

Where I'll stay extra coy
Cuz I learned as a boy
The concrete shadows of deceit

Yet isn't it neat
Unlike my mind or your sheets
I might could give a teat
Not to street where I treat

Dare I ask again
No weapon in hand
How I'd prefer to stand
A four-footed plan
To meet the eyes of this incredible man

Why Wonder

Why should I wonder
About the standstill in my brain
Mulling over the moments
Wishing to be less sane
When the tides run low
Thoughts lose all flight
Towering nothingness
Lack of delight
How that prison system wins
With its gun to my head
Curled up in the corner
Might as well be dead

But I'm not sad enough to cry
Don't care enough to try
A world that seems blank
Not batting an eye
No troubles worth caring
No visions worth sharing
Flightless bird she yells
Tucked in cozy
Her personal hells

So why should I wonder
That standstill to my brain

No moments to mull over
Not even insane
As the tides run out of oceans
Flight cycles is for the birds
Too tired to tower out
Guess I'm a coward now

Maladjusted

And it was then
Just like that
When she gave you away
A mere child
Of only eight

His heart winced
So very alone
Without much capital
But the strength to live on

As he did
The more of himself he hid
He was just a kid
Her heart was cut off
He was forced to bid

Unloved all the same
She resented his name
Beautiful boy
Devoid of all joy

Cries and screams
Not knowing what any of it means
Curled in a ball
Shouting inside empty walls

Bowing out

One day I might be ready
Ready for your love
When you're near me

Working on a rhythm to your right
A slim chance
Another fight
Don't matter when all you want is hands to
mend

That's how it is
What they'll say
How you'll smile most
As it fades away

Battles you faced the most
Troubled now
Just little kids
Hide your face
There's nothing left to forgive

Blue in the faced with;
Weak with such knees
Traveled about a bunch
Never knowing nothing

Saw something
Said anything
Knew it as before
You ever thought to walk away

Work it out
Stop calling
Hear me out
Doesn't want to talk about it
Never meant it
Heard it vomit
Heard it sin

Back out